Nevada

Jim Ollhoff

Visit us at
www.abdopublishing.com

Published by ABDO Publishing Company, 8000 West 78th Street, Suite 310, Edina,
Minnesota 55439 USA. Copyright ©2010 by Abdo Consulting Group, Inc. International
copyrights reserved in all countries. No part of this book may be reproduced in any
form without written permission from the publisher. The Checkerboard Library™ is a
trademark and logo of ABDO Publishing Company.

Printed in the United States.

Editor: John Hamilton
Graphic Design: Sue Hamilton
Cover Illustration: Neil Klinepier
Cover Photo: iStock

Manufactured with paper
containing at least 10%
post-consumer waste

Interior Photo Credits: Alamy, AP Images, Comstock, Corbis, David Olson, Getty,
Granger Collection, Great Reno Balloon Race, iStock Photo, Jeff Schiewe, John Hamilton,
Library of Congress, Mile High Maps, Mountain High Maps, Nellis Air Force Base, North
Wind Picture Archives, and One Mile Up.
Statistics: State population statistics taken from 2008 U.S. Census Bureau estimates.
City and town population statistics taken from July 1, 2007, U.S. Census Bureau
estimates. Land and water area statistics taken from 2000 Census, U.S. Census Bureau.

Library of Congress Cataloging-in-Publication Data

Ollhoff, Jim, 1959-
  Nevada / Jim Ollhoff.
      p. cm. -- (The United States)
  Includes index.
  ISBN 978-1-60453-663-8
  1. Nevada--Juvenile literature. I. Title.

F841.3.O45 2010
979.3--dc22

                              2008051719

Table of Contents

The Silver State

Nevada has a rich, Old West history. It is the home of gold rushes and silver mining. Its nickname, "The Silver State," is a reminder of its mining history.

Mountain men led brave settlers across the state toward the West Coast. Native Americans and pioneers did not always get along in Nevada.

The desert meets the mountains in Nevada. It's a land of stark desert beauty and high mountain forests.

Nevada is the seventh-largest state, but not many people live there. About three-fourths of the population lives in the cities of Las Vegas and Reno. The rest of the population is spread out in small towns.

Nevada has an exciting history. It's also a great place to live today.

Hoover Dam uses the power of the Colorado River to create electricity for the people of Nevada.

Quick Facts

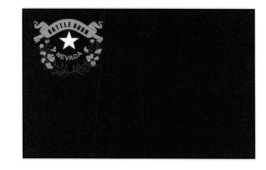

Name: From the Spanish language meaning "snow-covered," a reference to the snow-caps of the Sierra Nevada mountains.

State Capital: Carson City, population 54,939

Date of Statehood: October 31, 1864 (36th state)

Population: 2,600,167 (35th-most populous state)

Area (Total Land and Water): 110,561 square miles (286,352 sq km), 7th-largest state

Largest City: Las Vegas, population 558,880

Nicknames: Silver State, Sagebrush State, Battle-Born State

Motto: All For Our Country

State Bird: Mountain Bluebird

Sagebrush

Single-Leaf Piñon

Boundary Peak

Colorado River

Laughlin

NEVADA

State Flower: Sagebrush

State Tree: The Single-Leaf Piñon

State Song: "Home Means Nevada"

Highest Point: Boundary Peak, 13,140 ft (4,005 m)

Lowest Point: Colorado River, 479 ft (146 m)

Average July Temperature: 86°F (30°C) in the south, 70°F (21°C) in the north

Record High Temperature: 125°F in (52°C) Laughlin, on June 29, 1994

Average January Temperature: 43°F (6°C) in the south, 24°F (-4°C) in the north

Record Low Temperature: -50°F (-46°C) in San Jacinto, on January 8, 1937

Average Annual Precipitation: 4 in (10 cm) in the south and 10 in (25 cm) in the north

Number of U.S. Senators: 2

Number of U.S. Representatives: 3

U.S. Postal Service Abbreviation: NV

Geography

The Nevada desert.

Nevada is covered mostly by desert. To some people deserts are beautiful lands. They are full of high mountains, rocky valleys, and stark beauty. To other people, the land is hot and barren.

Nevada has few lakes and rivers. There is little underground water. This is a big concern as farms grow and cities get more people.

The early explorers and settlers struggled with the desert. It was an unknown land. Mistakes in the desert could be deadly.

Most of Nevada, and small parts of surrounding states, make up the Great Basin. A basin is an area where the rivers empty into lakes or ponds. None of the rivers in a basin empty into the ocean.

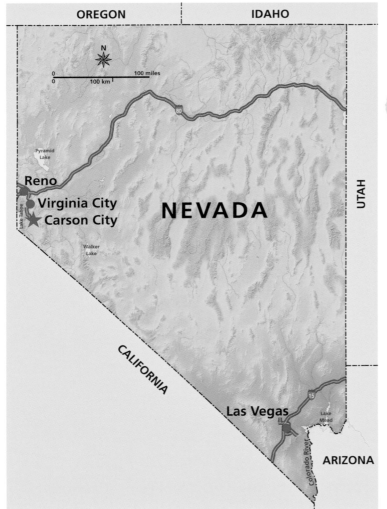

OREGON IDAHO

UTAH

NEVADA

Pyramid
Lake

Reno

Virginia City

Carson City

Lake Tahoe

Walker
Lake

CALIFORNIA

Las Vegas

Lake
Mead

Colorado River

ARIZONA

N

0   100 miles
0   100 km

80

15

Nevada's total
land and water
area is 110,561
square miles
(286,352 sq km).
It is the 7th-largest
state. The state
capital is Carson
City.

More than 30 mountain ranges cross the state, mostly going north and south. Many of the mountains formed about 15 million years ago. Large, moving pieces of the earth's crust pushed against each other. Sometimes the earth's crust pushed upwards, creating mountains.

Some of Nevada's mountains were formed by erupting volcanoes. The molten magma from inside the earth shot to the surface. This lava cooled and formed mountains.

Long ago, some of Nevada's mountains were formed by erupting volcanoes.

The state's most famous body of water is Lake Tahoe. It is the second-deepest lake in the United States, at 1,645 feet (501 m). It is on the border with California, just west of Carson City, Nevada. It is a popular tourist resort. People are drawn to the clear water and natural beauty. Mountains surround Lake Tahoe. People enjoy the nearby ski resorts and other outdoor attractions.

Nevada's famous Lake Tahoe.

A skier views Lake Tahoe.

The Colorado River weaves its way on the very southern part of the state. Two large lakes in the area are Pyramid Lake and Walker Lake. These two lakes are all that is left of a large, ancient sea that once covered much of Nevada.

Climate and Weather

Rain and moisture travel eastward over California. But the Sierra Nevada mountain range blocks much of the moisture before it gets to Nevada. So, much of the state is dry. Some parts of the state get as little as 4 inches (10 cm) of rain a year. In the mountains on the west side of the state, there is much more rain. It can rain 24 inches (61 cm) a year in the mountains.

A rainbow forms during a rain storm near Elko, Nevada.

In the northern part of the state, winters are long and cold. In January, the temperature averages

Several feet of snow blanket a man's car after a northern Nevada winter storm.

about 24 degrees Fahrenheit (-4°C). In July, in the northern part of the state, the average temperature is about 70 degrees Fahrenheit (21°C).

In the south side of the state, the winters are warm and short. In January, the average temperature is about 43 degrees Fahrenheit (6°C). In July, the average temperature is about 86 degrees Fahrenheit (30°C).

Plants and Animals

Even though much of Nevada is desert, there are still many plants and animals that are able to withstand the area's heat and lack of water. In the desert areas of Nevada, it is common to find mesquite, creosote, greasewood, many varieties of cactus, and yucca plants. Sagebrush and Joshua trees are also found in Nevada.

In the state's mountainous areas, there are forests. These forests have many different kinds of trees, such as pine, fir, spruce, juniper, and mountain mahogany.

More than 2,000 kinds of wildflowers grow in Nevada. Sagebrush is the official state flower.

Mountain lions, sometimes called cougars, live in Nevada. They like the rocks of the mountains, but these large cats can also be found in the desert.

Nevada's Red Rock Canyon area has some of the state's common plants, including Joshua trees, sagebrush, and greasewood plants.

Bighorn sheep, deer, and pronghorn antelope can be found in Nevada, often in the mountains. They are able to survive both the extremes in temperature, as well as the small amount of water there. Mountain beavers and black bears like the thick vegetation of the state's forests.

Smaller animals found in Nevada are rabbits, coyotes, and bobcats. Reptiles such as desert tortoises, geckos, and rattlesnakes live in the state.

Game birds such as the sage grouse, quail, and pheasant are found in Nevada. The mountain bluebird is the state bird. The bald eagle and types of hawks and owls can be found here. Roadrunners are native to the state.

Roadrunner

In the lakes, trout, bass, crappie, and catfish are common. The pikeminnow, the razorback sucker, and bonytail chub swim in the waters of the Colorado River.

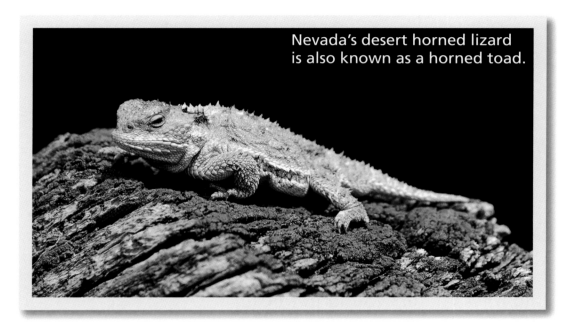

Nevada's desert horned lizard is also known as a horned toad.

Bighorn Sheep

Desert Tortoise

Coyote

History

People have lived in Nevada for a long time. The first people in the state were called Paleo-Indians, who arrived about 12,000 years ago.

By the late 1700s, several Native American tribes lived in the Nevada area. The Paiute lived in the west and southeast parts of the state. The Shoshone lived in northeastern Nevada. The Ute lived in a small part of eastern Nevada. The Mohave made their homes in the very south of Nevada.

Native Americans see the Transcontinental Railroad.

The first European to explore Nevada may have been Francisco Garcés. He was a missionary. He explored the area in 1775 or 1776. By 1825, trappers arrived to explore the state.

By 1830, the Old Spanish Trail was established. It was a route between Santa Fe, New Mexico, and Los Angeles, California. The trail crossed the southern tip of Nevada.

Beginning in 1843, John Frémont and a group of explorers began to map the area of Nevada. Frémont named the Carson River in honor of his friend, Kit Carson.

John Frémont explored and mapped parts of Nevada.

From 1846 to 1848, the United States fought a war with Mexico. The Mexican-American War resulted in the United States gaining a large section of land, including present-day Nevada.

The first European-American settlement in Nevada was in Genoa, south of Carson City, beginning in 1851.

In 1859, silver was discovered in Virginia City. The find was called the Comstock Lode. This mine had the first large vein of silver found in the United States. Gold was also discovered nearby. Treasure hunters rushed to the state. Mining camps sprang up quickly.

A cutaway view of the mines of the Comstock Lode at Virginia City, Nevada.

In 1864, President Abraham Lincoln realized that the wealth of minerals could greatly help the United States. Nevada's request for statehood was quickly accepted. On October 31, 1864, Nevada became the 36th state.

The years that followed had ups and downs for the state. There was tension between the miners and the cattle ranchers. When the price of silver declined, many mines had to close, creating ghost towns. The winters were harsh, which made cattle ranching difficult. The population of Nevada went down.

From 1905-1910, the town of Rhyolite, Nevada, was a booming gold town. By 1919, the gold had run out and the town was abandoned. Today, it is a ghost town.

Nevada's railroads helped miners, farmers, and ranchers move their products.

In the early 1900s, more minerals were discovered. Silver was found in Tonopah, copper was unearthed in Ely, and gold was discovered at Goldfield. As railroads were built, it cost less to ship the minerals. The railroads also helped ranchers and farmers.

The Great Depression of the 1930s hit Nevada hard. But leaders of Nevada decided on a way to bring money into the state. They created tourist attractions and resort areas. Areas like Las Vegas became famous for gambling and entertainment. The state of Nevada continues to rely on tourism, gaming, and entertainment for income.

In the 1950s, the United States military built huge bases in Nevada. This helped grow the economy. North of Las Vegas, the military began to test nuclear bombs. More than 100 nuclear bombs were tested. It wasn't yet known how dangerous nuclear bombs were. Scientists didn't understand the harmful effects of radiation and radioactive fallout. In the 1960s, the tests were moved underground. In 1992, testing stopped altogether.

A nuclear bomb explodes in the Nevada desert in 1952.

Did You Know?

Jedediah Smith was born in 1799. He was one of the most famous mountain men. The mountain men were explorers, hunters, trappers, traders, and expedition leaders. They lived off the land, often wearing clothes of animal skins.

Smith was the first white man to cross Nevada. He was the first white man to reach California overland. He was the first to scale the Sierra Nevada mountains. He was the first white explorer to reach Oregon by walking up the California coast. Smith traveled more in unknown territory than anyone else.

There were many dangers in the wilderness. Once, a bear attacked him. It bit Smith in the head, tearing off his ear and part of his scalp.

But this was one tough mountain man. Smith told a friend how to sew his ear and scalp back together.

Jedediah Smith died in 1831, probably after a fight with several Comanche warriors.

Jedediah Smith was the first white man to cross Nevada.

People

Tennis player **Andre Agassi** (1970-) was born in Las Vegas, Nevada. Agassi grew into one of the most famous players in professional tennis history. He charmed audiences with his unusual antics and

hard play. He won his first professional tournament in 1987, and continued to win tournaments after that. Overcoming a number of injuries, he was eventually rated number one in the world. Agassi retired from professional tennis in 2006. He now spends time with his charitable foundation, which helps at-risk kids.

Author **Sarah Winnemucca** (1844? – 1891) was the daughter of Chief Winnemucca of the Paiute tribe. Sarah could speak five languages by the time she was 14. In 1871, she worked as a translator for the Bureau of Indian Affairs. She became the first Native American woman to publish a book in English. Sarah wrote a history of how her people, the Paiutes, came into contact with explorers and settlers. Sarah Winnemucca gave many speeches to try to help her people. She died of tuberculosis in 1891.

Wovoka (1856?-1932) was a Paiute shaman, or religious leader. He was born south of Carson City sometime around the year 1856. Wovoka founded the famous Ghost Dance movement. In 1889, he claimed to have a vision that told him that God would restore the Native Americans to their ancestral lands. He said that members of the tribes should live right and perform the Ghost Dance. Wovoka thought that the Native American uprising would be peaceful. However, others used his teachings to create warfare. Wovoka went by the name of Jack Wilson when working with whites. He is buried in Schurz, Nevada.

Pat Nixon (1912-1993) was born in Ely, Nevada. She grew up to become the wife of the 37th president of the United States. Her family moved to California when Pat was a young girl. She graduated from college and met a young lawyer named Richard Nixon. They were married in 1940. She helped her husband as he entered politics. Richard Nixon became president in 1969. As first lady, Pat urged people to help in their community. She spoke often about volunteering in schools, hospitals, and nursing homes. Pat Nixon died of lung cancer in 1993.

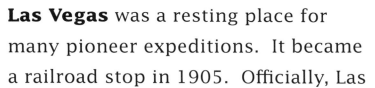

Cities

The area that would become **Las Vegas** was a resting place for many pioneer expeditions. It became a railroad stop in 1905. Officially, Las Vegas became a city in 1911. Today, the city has a population of 558,880 people. However, by including the surrounding suburbs and towns, nearly half the people of Nevada live in the area. Las Vegas benefited from the completion of the Hoover Dam in 1935. The dam provides cheap hydroelectric power. A number of colleges are located in Las Vegas, including the University of Nevada. Gambling and entertainment have made Las Vegas a famous vacation spot for tourists.

Carson City is named after the famous mountain man, Kit Carson. Like many towns in Nevada, it was established during the early days of mining in the 1850's. When miners found silver nearby, Carson City began to grow. Today, it has a population of 54,939, and is the capital of Nevada. Western Nevada College is one of the colleges that serves the area.

Kit Carson

Carson City was named after mountain man Kit Carson.

Reno was an important stopping point on the California Trail. When silver was discovered in Virginia City in 1859, Reno became the place where treasure hunters veered off the trail to go south to Virginia City. Services and business, such as hotels and restaurants, sprang up. When the railroads were built, Reno became an established town in 1868. Today, the population is about 214,853.

Virginia City is located southeast of Reno. Gold and silver were discovered in the area in 1859. The famous Comstock Lode silver strike brought thousands of people to the city. The mineral discoveries and great wealth helped lead Nevada to statehood in 1864. Today, Virginia City is an official national historic landmark. The population is about 1,500, but each year more than 2 million visitors come to see Virginia City's many museums and popular historical attractions.

Actors in Virginia City.

Transportation

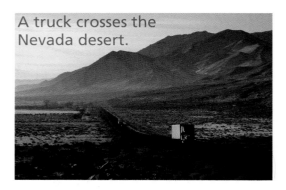
A truck crosses the Nevada desert.

Interstate I-80 goes east and west on the northern side of Nevada. It goes through the cities of Elko, Winnemucca, and Reno. I-80 follows roughly the route of the first Transcontinental Railroad. Interstate I-70 cuts across the south side of the state through Las Vegas. Nevada has almost 40,000 miles (64,374 km) of public streets and highways, and 560 miles (901 km) of interstate. There are 1,423 road bridges in Nevada.

Railroads are still important in Nevada. The state has almost 2,000 miles (3,219 km) of railroads.

A plane takes off from McCarran International Airport in Las Vegas. The Luxor hotel and casino can be seen in the background

Air travel is important because Nevada is such a large state. Both Las Vegas and Reno have international airports. Nevada has six commercial airports and almost 100 other airfields and heliports.

Natural Resources

The United States federal government owns about 85 percent of the land in Nevada. This land

An EA-6 Prowler takes off from Nellis Air Force Base.

includes the military operations of Nellis Air Force Base and Fallon Naval Air Station.

Nevada has some of the richest mineral deposits in the country. The state is the leading producer of barite (used in paint) and mercury. Nevada continues to mine silver and gold. Sand, gravel, and gypsum are also mined.

Oil drilling has been going on since 1907. In 1954, oil was discovered southwest of Ely, Nevada. Today, oil comes from several places in the state. Scientists think much more oil is located there.

Nevada has about 5.9 million acres (2.4 million ha) of farmland. Much land is used for grazing cattle. Dairy and poultry farms have also grown recently.

A cowboy herds free-range cattle through blooming sagebrush.

Industry

In the late 1800s and early 1900s, mining and agriculture were the

Fireworks explode over the Las Vegas skyline.

most important parts of the Nevada economy. That is no longer true. Today, manufacturing and government are very important. The most important part of all is tourism and the entertainment industry. In Las Vegas, Reno, and in other places, there is 24-hour-a-day gambling. Casinos, nightclubs, performances, and restaurants bring in a lot of money to the state.

Another part of tourism is the income from the national parks and national recreation areas. Places like Lake Tahoe and Lake Mead provide recreational areas for tourists.

Nevada businesses manufacture many kinds of clay and glass products. Printing and food production are important businesses, as well.

A climber atop Wheeler Peak in Nevada's Great Basin National Park.

Thousands of military personnel are stationed in Nevada. These military operations provide a big part of the state's economy.

Sports

There are no major league sports teams in Nevada. There are minor league and development teams, mostly in Las Vegas.

College sports teams are important in Nevada. The University of Nevada-Las Vegas basketball team has been a powerhouse. People follow high school sports as well.

Las Vegas and Reno host martial arts championships and professional boxing title bouts.

Nevada has a number of beautiful recreational areas. Many of these places have hiking trails, biking, climbing, and horseback riding. Hunting and wildlife viewing are popular. Golf is enjoyed in many areas.

The area of Lake Tahoe is especially popular for all kinds of recreational activities. From hang gliding to snowboarding to jet-skiing, there is plenty to do around Lake Tahoe.

A hang glider soars over the Nevada landscape.

Entertainment

Many people from Nevada value the state's Old West heritage. Each May, Las Vegas hosts a festival called Helldorado Days. People wear Western clothes and enjoy Old West activities, including parades and concerts.

Reno celebrates the 1950s in August with classic cars and rock 'n roll. The Great Reno Balloon Race is one of the biggest hot air balloon rallies in the United States. Reno also holds one of the largest rodeos in the West.

One of the most unusual festivals is the Winnemucca Mule Races. It involves races from mules that have been cloned by scientists.

Reno and Las Vegas have a number of galleries that feature traditional Native American art.

Performing arts and symphony orchestras are popular. The biggest entertainment center is Las Vegas. With casinos, theaters, and big-name performers, Las Vegas is the center of entertainment for the state, and perhaps the entire country.

The Great Reno Balloon Race features more than 100 hot-air balloons.

Timeline

Late 1700s—Paiute, Shoshone, Mohave, and Ute live in the Nevada area.

1775-1776—The first European arrives, Francisco Garcés.

1825—Trappers explore the state.

1830—The Old Spanish Trail is established.

1843—John Frémont and a group of explorers begin to map the area of Nevada.

1848—The United States obtains Nevada from Mexico in the Mexican-American War.

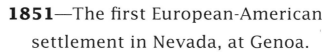

Virginia City

1851—The first European-American settlement in Nevada, at Genoa.

1859—Silver is discovered in Virginia City.

1864—Nevada becomes the 36th state.

1940s—Tourist attractions, including gambling and resort areas, are built.

1950s—The U.S. military builds huge bases in Nevada. Nuclear bomb testing begins.

1962—The military ends nuclear testing above aground.

1997—Andy Green sets the world supersonic land speed record of 763 mph (1,228 kph) in the Thrust SSC at Black Rock Desert.

Glossary

Basin—An area where rivers do not drain into the ocean.

Bureau of Indian Affairs—An agency of the United States government in charge of protecting Native American rights and managing their land. It was originally created in 1824.

Comstock Lode—An extremely rich find of silver and gold in the Virginia Mountains of western Nevada. Found in 1859, it is named after one of the original finders, Henry Comstock.

Great Depression—Beginning in 1929 and lasting into the mid 1930s, this was a time when the United States economy was bad. Many businesses failed and millions of people lost their jobs. Few people had money to spend.

Mexican-American War—In the 1840s, fighting broke out between the Mexican citizens in the southwest and the settlers from the United States. The angry Mexican government told the United States to get its Navy and Army out of California. The United States refused, which led to war. The Mexican-American War lasted from 1846 until 1848.

Old Spanish Trail—A route between Sante Fe, New Mexico, and Los Angeles, California. The trail crossed the southern tip of Nevada.

Paleo-Indians—The first residents of Nevada. Most people believe these were the ancestors of the modern Native American tribes.

Transcontinental Railroad—The first railroad line that stretched across the United States. It traveled east and west across the north part of Nevada.

Tuberculosis—A sometimes fatal disease that most often affects the lungs, but may spread to other areas of the body. The disease is caused by bacteria, and is commonly spread through coughing.

Index